FOR SALE BY OWNER

It's Not Rocket Science;
Just Follow the Rules

Jeni Temen

ISBN: 978-1-7345015-0-6

Library of Congress Control Number: 2020900517

Printed in Cedarville, California, USA by R Money Club

The publisher has strived to be as accurate and complete as possible in the creation of this book.

This book is not intended for use as a source of legal, health, medical, business, accounting, or financial advice. All readers are advised to seek the services of competent professionals in legal, health, medical, business, accounting, and financial fields.

The advice and strategies found within may not be suitable for every situation. This work is sold with the understanding that neither the author nor the publisher is held responsible for the results accrued from the advice in this book.

While all attempts have been made to verify information provided for this publication, the publisher assumes no responsibility for errors, omissions, or contrary interpretation of the subject matter herein.

Because of the dynamic nature of the Internet, any web addresses or links contained in this book may have changed since publication of this book and may no longer be valid.

For more information, visit https://www.RMoneyClub.com/

For bulk book orders, contact Jeni Temen at Coach@RMoneyClub.com

Dedication

This book is dedicated to my daughter Karin, for always reminding me to share my knowledge with others.

Table of Contents

Introduction

Are you thinking about selling your home without a realtor and not sure where to start?

Have you started to ask questions about the process and what you have received is pitches from agents to sell your home for you...so they make money?

Are you frustrated with the information you have found and you're looking for expert advice on how to proceed with the process?

This book is for you!

There is a lot of confusing information out there about the process. The focus of this book is to help you forget the fear of selling your home and put the profit in your pocket!

It is a short, easy-to-understand guide, written by a real estate professional with nearly 20 years· experience in the real world, helping hundreds of clients both buy and sell their homes, land, farms, ranches and investment properties.

Inside you'll discover the entire process of selling a house for the most money, with or without a realtor. At some point, if you decide that listing with an agent is the best path forward, this book includes information on how to choose the right agent and make it work for your situation.

Read the entire book first and then decide if you would like to proceed with selling your home and how you want to do it.

The focus of this book is on selling a **residential** property and includes the common process steps for any residential property, including ones with wells, septic systems, and acreage. Also included is information about how to sell with owner carry terms and what is needed for reverse mortgages. See the back of the book for more information on these two situations.

If you want to sell a commercial building, I strongly recommend engaging a commercial Realtor, since selling commercial property requires an additional certification. Find someone who is very active in the area where the building is located.

For selling a business, I strongly recommend a Realtor with a Business Broker license, because that is a totally different game.

At the end of the book you will find details on each form you should have and how to fill them out.

A few extra notes

I've studied various schools of Feng Shui and Numerology and actively used both in each and every real estate transaction, for both myself and my clients. Feng Shui is the language of harmony. When you buy a house that is out of harmony with your own energy, you can lose money, get sick, or have something else that is troubling happen.

I've included both Feng Shui tips I use to sell a house, which is vital information for successfully selling your home. These tips are for general use. If you'd like a personalized analysis, email me at coach@RMoney-Club.com or check out www.RMoneyClub.com

The tips inside this book are all tied to how to sell a house, **not** how to buy a home. If you would like to know more about buying a home to support you, your family, and your lifestyle, check out my other book: *"How to Buy a Home that Makes You Happy!*

Chapter 1

IMPORTANT THINGS TO KNOW

Know that a "Sale by Owner" means just that: By **Owner.**

The owner is the person(s) recorded on the title, not a brother or parents or relatives or friends. Real Estate is a regulated industry and if you decide you now know enough to sell a house where your name is not on the title, you could be subject to a lawsuit for "acting without a license." The fines are huge. Don't do it.

If you get an idea to pay people who are not Realtors or Attorneys to help you sell your house, rethink. Don't do it. You can get in legal trouble.

Continue reading this book until the end and you will learn to follow the entire process.

You might get the idea to hire an attorney to help you sell the house so that you don't need to use a Realtor. Be aware that you could end up paying an attorney a whole lot more money than you would pay a Realtor, and they might not know the real estate sales business as much as you expect. I have represented attorneys

in the past while they were selling their own homes. If you feel you need an attorney, make sure they are educated in real estate sales.

Keep making mortgage payments until closing.

You will get reimbursed at close of escrow if you over-paid. This is important because if the sale doesn't go through for whatever reason, you will be in default, and that can ruin your credit big time.

Keep your insurance until the day after closing. Keep your utilities on until the day of closing .

Chapter 2

Make the Decision to Sell

The first and most important step is to make sure that you, and whoever lives with you, truly want to sell the house. This is not a joke: if anyone who owns the property holds on to it in their heart, the house will not sell. This also counts for cases when you say, "I will sell it if I get a certain amount." It will not sell. So, take this seriously and make sure everyone is on the same page. Don't waste your time and energy if someone is holding on to it.

Now that you have disconnected from the property emotionally, sell it and move on to a different place. Congratulations!

Chapter 3

CLEAN AND DECLUTTER

If the house is vacant:

If you don't have a choice and the house is vacant, please make sure it is clean, especially the front entry and the front door.

Clean windows and repair broken screens and broken blinds.

Make sure the doors and knobs are clean and open smoothly.

Clean all sinks.

Put a new, dark and clean doormat in front of the entry door.

On each side of the door, place a red or terracotta pot of flowers/plants. You can even place fake plants if they look real.

Inside the house, put some fresh flower vases in each room. Again, if you can't do real plants, use fake, but they need to be clean and look real. The intention is to add life to a vacant home.

Use an apple cinnamon scent in several places, but make sure it is not too strong. An overpowering smell of any kind will rush the potential buyers out with no interest. Scented candles can do it.

Put a vase with flowers or colorful marbles on the right side of your house, meaning, when you open your main entry door, the corner of the house farthest to your right. Inside the vase or marble dish, put a note that says, "I wish for this house to sell fast and for the most money." Do the same thing in the farthest left corner of your house.

If your house is NOT vacant, and you still live in it full or part time:

The home and property need to be cleaned and organized.

Most personal items need to be removed.

If you have a lot of family photos or awards and accomplishments framed on the walls, please take them off and pack them away. People get distracted easily by other's belongings and start making the strangest assumptions. You don't want that. You want a buyer to concentrate on the house and property, not on your personal items.

Fill holes in the wall if you have any and touch up the paint, but please use matching paint or you will make the walls look worse.

Take as much furniture out as you can. The more space the better.

If you don't have a storage room, it might be a good idea to lease a storage container or unit either at the property or in town.

Pack your things and organize them in the garage, but keep in mind that buyers will often look at the garage first. Don't clutter the garage with stuff from the house!

Clean windows, replace broken blinds, replace broken screens on windows and doors, and fix leaking faucets.

Determine which appliances will stay and which will not.

Determine what fixtures will stay.

Everything attached to the house needs to stay. Sometimes people choose to replace expensive chandeliers and other fixtures. You can do that but do it prior to showing the house to a potential buyer.

This is the best time to decide what stays and what goes. This counts for trees, shrubs and plants around the property as well. Potted plants can go, but only with the buyer's consent if they were still on the property when showing the house.

Make sure you have something in each of the following colors in your home, especially in the main room in the house: Yellow, black, red, green, and purple. You can have a few pillows or put out a vase with flowers with all the colors.

Do the same in the very back left corner of your house, no matter what room that is. Using the main entry of your house, look and discover the far-left corner at the back of your house.

If you can't put all the colors in a vase, be sure to include something else with all the colors, especially gold and purple, even if it is just a bowl of marbles. This attracts money.

When you put the colors in the far-left room, be sure to place your intention to sell the house fast and for as much money as possible into the room as well. That means, write on a piece of paper, "I want to sell this house fast and get the most money for it."

Hide that paper anywhere in that corner, meaning the back left of your house. Do the same thing in the right corner of your house.

The main road to the property needs to be very well marked and visible. What I mean by that is, many homes have a driveway where you don't know where it will end. If that's the case, put something in place that marks the driveway, like lights or even rocks marking the driveway all the way to the main door.

As I mentioned in the section on a vacant property, put a fresh, new (or clean) mat at the front doorstep and one potted plant on each side. The mat should prefer-ably be black and the pots red.

The door needs to be clean, and if it needs a new coat of paint, do that. The knob needs to be clean. All the doorknobs in the house need to be, too.

Note: No one likes greasy, dirty doorknobs. This is an instant turn off.

If your house needs work, whether deferred maintenance or updates, make a list and get estimates to find out how much it will cost before you jump into doing the work. Many times, it is much easier to let the buyers decide what they want to have done and what they don't. If the property and home is clean and organized, you will find cooperating buyers more easily.

Repairs, on the other hand, like plumbing issues, peeling paint, missing shingles, broken windows or doors, etc., must be taken care of.

If you have a lawn, make it look good. If you have sprinklers, make sure they work or disclose if they don't.

If you have children, make sure they also have few things around the house. This is especially hard with small kids, but it is necessary for a faster sale.

If you have pets, remove all litter boxes and animal cages.

Remove clutter from countertops in the kitchen and bathrooms, organize the laundry room, and clean the fridge. Just about everyone looking at a house will open the refrigerator. I don't know why, but they always do.

If you have rooms painted in various colors, especially if bright, it is a good idea to paint the walls in a neutral color. White does the trick. People don't like bright colors when they buy a house.

OK, the property is clean and organized, and all emotions are cooperating with selling the house. Go to the next step.

Chapter 4

GATHER ALL PAPERWORK

Paperwork you need on hand before you list your house:

You need the property's recorded documents from the city or county. You should be able to access the recorder's website and print the forms by the APN (Area Parcel Number) or your name. You might still have that from the time you bought it.

You also need a Seller Real Property Disclosure. You need to disclose everything and anything that might not work properly on the house and property. More disclosure is better. It will keep you out of a lawsuit.

At the end of the book you will find a few suggested forms you can use.

Any addition or remodel to the property needs to be disclosed, including if it was built/remodeled with or without a licensed contractor.

If it was you doing the work, say, "owner remodeled," or, "repaired by owner." Do not be afraid to disclose!

You need to know how many square feet the house has and how many the property has. You can find that information in the recorded documents.

Keep those numbers in your file, you will need them for answering questions and for the closing.

If you have a homeowner's association, or several, you need the names of the associations and the cost of the dues.

Disclose! Disclose! Disclose! Don't get the idea that selling "as is" is going to keep you out of courts. "As is" only helps you if you disclosed before escrow closed. This counts if you use a Realtor as well.

You can print a sale contract for your particular state at the link below. Have this contract on hand and learn what else you need to have in place for a successful sale.

https://www.lawdepot.com/contracts/real-estate-purchase-agreement

At the end of the book I'll explain how to fill out a generic contract. Once you have an offer, you can use the above link and enter all of your particular details. You can also write it all by yourself using the contract form details at the back of the book.

Chapter 5

WHAT PRICE TO LIST

Now is the time to decide if you want to use a Realtor or if you want to proceed with For Sale by Owner. Keep on reading and you will proceed either way successfully.

The second most important step after you make the decision to sell is to price the home correctly.

Pricing a property is not about how much you paid for it plus how much you added to remodel (That only works in commercial property cases and, very rarely, in some short sale cases.)

The way you price the property is by determining how it will appraise.

You can order an appraisal if you feel so inclined, but that can be a waste of about $400-$600 (sometimes even more), because that appraisal is only for your gratification.

A buyer will have an appraisal ordered by the loan company that's required by the buyer's lender.

You can go on the internet, to sites like Zillow.com or Realtor.com or Redfin.com, and search your zip code and the pricing on neighborhood homes in your area. Check all three and see what price they would recommend on your own address.

You can use that suggested sell price to begin with.

Have you ever wondered why you so often see a price that ends with 9? Or 99? Like $19.99? Well, there is a reason for that. The number 9 is the luckiest number in Feng Shui. You should price your house so that the last number is 9. E.g. $239,999 and not $240,000.

Chapter 6

Put Up a Sign

Go to Home Depot or any other hardware store and buy a **For Sale By Owner** sign, or you can make one yourself. Make sure it is big enough, at least as big as a Realtor sign. If your community allows, you can make it bigger.

Note: If you live within an association with bylaws, make sure they don't have restrictions on how and where to put a For Sale sign. Sometimes they have requirements on what kind of sign, the size, colors and where it can be placed. Don't skip this step, associations can remove your sign without a notice.

It is very important that your sign states, "By Owner," and has your phone number on it.

Place the sign on the right side of the driveway entry. Put flowers on the bottom of the sign or add colorful balloons.

I suggest you keep one flyer attached to the For-Sale sign under a plastic cover. Have your phone number written and visible from a distance on the flyer and suggest calling for an appointment. Most interested buyers will take a photo of your flyer with the phone.

If you have a flyer box with a lot of flyers in it, expect them to go really quickly. Some people might just empty the box for no reason. It could be a lot of wasted money.

People want to know the price, how many bedrooms, how many baths and how much land.

Don't go by the idea that the price should not be put on the sign. That's wrong. People want to know if it is in their price range. You don't want buyers who are polite and go through the entire show and tell, but when they hear the price realize it is way more than they can ever afford. That tactic only worked before 2008 when people bought homes 2 or 3 times pricier than they could afford by merely stating their income; no proof was needed. Today, buyers have a price limit.

This is all you need to list on the flyer: Price, number of bedrooms, number of baths, how much land and phone number.

Everything else is crowded and not needed at this time. The phone number to call and the price need to be very visible to someone who doesn't want to get out of the car.

To make flyers you can use:

http://www.Etsy.com

http://www.ideastage.com

http://www.vistaprint.com

A Special Bonus from Jeni

Now that you have your copy of *For Sale By Owner*, you are on your way to understanding exactly how you can sell your home for the most money you can get at the time you want to sell it, with or without a Realtor. You can now forget the fear of selling your home and put the profit in your own pocket!

You'll also receive the special bonus I created to add to your toolkit ... The *FSBO Toolkit*, which includes:

- List of key resources links you will need for success in selling your home (with links for direct access)
- Seller Real Property Disclosure form
- Special pricing on classes and offerings. See below for details.

This *FSBO Toolkit* is offered as a special bonus to this book's readers, and you can claim it for free here:

https://www.rmoneyclub.com/toolkit

Did you know that you can begin real estate investing, even if you don't have a lot of money? No get rich fast scheme...just sound, professional coaching to help you achieve your financial independence. Email me at Coach@RMoneyClub.com for your special pricing.

Did you know that interest rates on any loan is directly tied to your credit report? Optimize your credit with a credit repair class. Email me at Coach@RMoneyClub.com for your special pricing.

Did you know that Feng Shui in your home is an invisible influence on your health, wealth, and overall happiness? Order a personalize Feng Shui analysis with special pricing. Just go to https://www.rmoneyclub.com/.

I'm in your corner. Let me know if I can help further.

Here's to the successful sale of your home!

Best,
Jeni

Chapter 7

LIST ON ZILLOW AND SOCIAL MEDIA

First, take pictures of the property to have handy when you start listing. You need a minimum of 20 photos: Indoor, outdoor and property pictures.

Make sure you don't take pictures of disorganized areas, like a kitchen full of dirty dishes, laundry rooms with laundry, or open toilet seats. Look at your pictures with the eye of a buyer and see if you like what you see.

If you have the means to pay for a professional photographer, do so. You can ask a local Realtor who they use for their listings and you'll get some names of photographers. There are some national companies you can call and find out if they have local photographers. If you have a property with a lot of land, I suggest drone photography. That will cost you some money but is worth every penny.

You can check your local homes for sale and see who uses drone photography. Prices vary by location. It could be $200.00 or $500.00 or sometimes more.

Here are some national companies. They usually have various packages that can include drone, too.

https://visualprophotography.com/

https://cs3design.com/nationwide-photography/real-estate/

https://www.bark.com/en/us/

Log in to Zillow.com and start listing the property on the For Sale By Owner tab. It is free. https://www.zillow.com/listing

You need to create an account and follow the prompts. If you have any problems, contact customer service at Zillow and they will help you. Contact them through their customer service email; it works.

Zillow allows you to include a video, but it has to be done live and after the listing is accepted and published. Be ready to take a video that very day for better results. You can use your cell phone for the video, and Zillow explains it very well and makes it easy.

Describe the property, concentrating on what the best use of it would be. Do not use terms like, "family friendly," or, "kid friendly."

Do not violate the Fair Housing Act! Take this seriously or you can get seriously fined!

Here is the link to learn more: https://www.hud.gov/program_offices/fair_housing_equal_opp/fair_housing_rights_and_obligations

Make sure you include a description of the city and state where the property is located. E.g. "This home in Wonderland, about 20 miles north of Dixieland, NY, is a well maintained 3BR," and so on. Most listings don't say that, and for someone who is searching the net, it is hard to understand where the property is located. Think as a buyer from out of town when you describe your home.

If your area has anything new that offers new area growth, mention that in the description after you describe your property. E.g. "Tesla just moved their manufacturing plant to the area."

If you have social media accounts, list the property and add your Zillow link.

Now the property is on the market. What else can you do to attract a buyer, not just viewers?

Let's apply some basic Feng Shui. You don't need to believe in Feng Shui; it just works. It's good to know a few tips to use to your advantage.

You need to take the home address and write it down. E.g. 164. Just the number, not the street name.

Add each number and reduce it to a single digit. E.g. 1+6+4=11, now add 1+1=2. This house is a 2 house.

So, here is the breakdown of each number in numerology. You will need some additional numbers for this step, and you can cut them out of paper. You need to place the number I'm suggesting respectively behind the front door. No need for it to be visible; no need to explain it to anyone. I would place mine in the same color the door is, on the door, inside the house with scotch tape.

A number 1 house- put number 8

A number 2 house- put number 7

A number 3 house- put two number 3

A number 4 house- put two number 1 and one number 3

A number 5 house- put one number 1 and one number 3

A number 6 house- put one number 3

A number 7 house- put one number 2

A number 8 house- put two number 1

A number 9 house- put one number 9

So, knowing the above info, be careful when you advertise. E.g. don't say, "this is a house number 7," and so on. Most people have no idea what that is, and you don't want to violate the Fair Housing Act. See Fair Housing at the end of this book.

Again, this information is not to be used to discriminate!

Anyone who wants to buy the house should be given the opportunity to do so.

This numerology tactic is only to be used to sell a home, not to buy.

When you're ready to buy or rent a new home, read my other book *"How to Buy a Home that Makes You Happy."*

From time to time, agents might come and tell you they can do a better job than you can. Now is not the time to stop what you're doing and turn it over. If you followed the steps and didn't overprice the property, you are doing a great job. The only difference is that the listing is not on Realtor.com. That is no longer as important as it was before Zillow arrived. The only way you can have a listing on Realtor.com is with an agent. Some companies allow agents to list FSBOs in the MLS for a low fee. This might be something you want to consider if they do it for less than $200.00. They might also tell you that a Realtor won't bring you an offer if it is not listed with a pro. Not true! A professional will bring you an offer if they have someone interested, and they will ask you for a certain commission. You would have to pay the Realtor the buyer's normal commission, but you can decide how much you want to pay. Negotiate with the agent, even if they tell you the commission is not negotiable. Not true! Commissions are always negotiable. **Know that an agent bringing you a buyer will ONLY represent the buyer, not you.**

Do NOT agree to buyer and seller representation!

What you can do is ask the agent nicely if they would agree to do an open house. Tell them if they bring a buyer, you will pay a Realtor fee. Don't agree with any amount just yet. Wait until you receive an offer and then negotiate.

You might be persuaded by" For Sale By Owner" website companies to list with them. They will tell you it is "free." It's not! You will pay close to $500.00 and will get persuaded to list with one of their agents. If you want to sell with an agent, use a local agent who knows your area and local rules and regulations. Also, if you want to sell with an agent, finish reading this book and then make your decision.

Going on, have the property disclosure handy to show any interested buyer. Most sellers are afraid of this step, but that's wrong. Don't be afraid. It shows that you don't hide things and makes a buyer instantly comfortable, even if the list is five pages long. Have a copy ready to give out, but only to someone who expresses interest and asks for it.

Chapter 8

SHOWINGS AND OPEN HOUSES

Once you're ready to show the house, make sure you don't have any prescription medication in any accessible cabinets. This is very important. Many people pretend to be buyers just to go use your bathroom and steal your meds. Have your medications locked or away from the property.

As I already mentioned, house and property need to be clean and decluttered for all showings.

Open window coverings, air the house out, turn off the TV, unless it is playing soft and quiet music, turn all lights on, and have all pets out.

I don't suggest open houses. You don't want to OPEN your house to whoever. In today's world, it is too dangerous and is only a way for an agent to get leads on new buyers. You don't need that. In the case of a Realtor wanting to do an open house for you, go for it. Let them do it. They're trained to do open houses but be there and watch what happens.

Do not assume that you are represented just because a Realtor is in your house. You are not, unless you sign a contract.

A Realtor will do an open house because they realize you will buy another house and they can serve you as a buyer's agent. I'll teach you how to handle the home buyer part in my book, *"How to Buy a Home that Makes You Happy!"*

When you have a showing, DO NOT volunteer more info. The property disclosure has all necessary info, don't talk about why you're moving or any personal info. Let them look, and if asked questions, be friendly but brief. Don't give a buyer a reason to know you really need to sell fast, but also don't tell them you have time and need not sell. Less is better at this time. Remember you're disclosing everything in the Seller Real Property Disclosure.

Be polite and give them your contact info.

If you have a surveillance camera, have a sign suggesting that or tell people outright, so that you are in compliance with state recording laws. Check your state requirements on this link.

https://www.upcounsel.com/audio-surveillance-laws-by-state

If you have the property on the market for 60 days and you see a lot of views and very few, or none, "saved the search" on the websites you have it listed, your price is too high. Lower the price a little, not aggressively, but something like $1,000.

You might have to do this a few times if you don't receive any offers. Wait a week and lower the price again if nothing changes. Price always matters.

If a showing goes well and they express interest, ask if they are pre-qualified or how they are intending to pay. Most people don't have a prequalification letter when they look at houses. Most lenders say, "Go find a house and then I'll give you the letter." The prequalification letter needs to be written for that specific house and price.

Chapter 9

YOU RECEIVED AN OFFER, NOW WHAT?

The scenario can be either or:

1- An agent brings you an offer.

2- You have an interested buyer without an agent who wants to write an offer but doesn't know how to.

If you receive an offer from an agent:

The agent will bring in the offer and ask you for a commission.

Review the offer with the agent and negotiate the commission amount if you don't like what they asked for. That agent will only represent the buyer. If you like the offer, accept it and the agent will do the rest.

No agent involved:

At the end of this book you have an explanation of a generic sell contract. Every state might have a different contract, but the basics are similar.

First, ask the buyer to give you a prequalification letter from the lender. If they don't have it, let them get it within 48 business hours. You need not dismiss that buyer, just put it in the contract.

If the buyer tells you it will be all cash, you will want proof of funds within 48 hours. Proof of funds can be a letter from the bank stating that buyer has sufficient funds to close the escrow on a property at the particular price. You can accept the offer and have that as a contingency.

You can also use a simple handwritten offer that addresses all necessary points (see back of the book). The escrow company will take it from there and finish the transaction. If the buyer prefers a particular escrow company, you can accept that. If not, choose the company you used when you bought the house. It makes it easier for the title search, but with no difference in price. In the rare case where you have a simple hand-written contract and an escrow officer tells you she/he can't work with such a contract, choose a different officer.

The contract needs to address:

Parcel number of the property (you will find this in the recorded documents or in the tax statement that you receive every year) listed as APN# 003-222-54.

Property address. Owner(s) name. Buyer(s) name. Purchase price. Property tax amount.

If you have an association, the cost of the dues.

Inspections - who does what and when (see back of book on inspections).

Repairs - how much you will pay. I always put a cap. Close of escrow date - usually 45 days, but you can ask the buyer when they think they want to close.

Earnest money deposit to open escrow (do not sign the contract if the buyer doesn't want to pay an earnest money deposit). The earnest money deposit is part of the selling price, not an additional amount, and is usually just $1000.00. Be aware that the earnest money deposit is to be refunded if escrow doesn't go through, even if the contract specifies "non-refundable." It will not stand in court if the buyer wants it back and will cost you a lot more money to go to court.

Buyer needs to specify how much money down they will pay (10%, 20%) and what kind of loan they are getting. The prequalification letter will specify that, but your contract needs to address the loan.

- Who will pay for what inspections
- Who will pay for what repairs
- How long the buyer has to complete inspections
- Who will pay for escrow
- When the escrow should be closed

It is important to know a few facts about a buyer's loan because it can affect your bottom line. You don't need to study all loans right now, but, instead, make sure you ask the buyer to put you in contact with their loan officer. Ask the loan officer if you need to give any concessions. Put that in writing. I'm saying this because some loans require a seller to pay for certain inspections, even for closing costs. This can be very costly to you. At the end of the book I'll list some common loans.

Details of the offer received

Use this page to make notes of all the details of the offer received so you can compare it to the information above. Identify anything that is missing.

_____

_____

_____

_____

_____

_____

_____

_____

_____

_____

_____

_____

_____

_____

_____

_____

_____

_____

_____

_____

_____

_____

_____

Chapter 10

NEGOTIATE AND ACCEPT OFFER

Once you receive an offer, the first thing to do is calculate your numbers and get an approximate net. If you don't know how to do that, the escrow officer can help you. If you don't have one yet, go to a calculator. Here is one from Western Title:

https://www.westerntitle.com/ecc

Once you got an approximate net, sleep on it. Never respond same day. If you wake up next day and feel good about it, take it. If the offer is off, write a counter-offer (see the back of this book).

Counter with either the price higher or some inspections to be paid by buyers.

Some buyers ask for the seller to pay for all inspections. That's negotiable.

Some buyers ask for the seller to give them money back at escrow. I wouldn't do that.

You can ask for a higher asking price or pay for some inspections.

Use the calculator for each option and see what gives you the best outcome. It won't be exact but will give you a good idea of if you are way off or about right.

When you write a counteroffer, you are just sending the counter to buyers, not the whole contract.

You don't sign the contract until all parties are in agreement. The buyer might come back with a different counteroffer, and this might go back and forth a few times. Once all parties agree, all contract pages need to be signed. If no agreement is reached, you will have to find a new buyer. Don't get discouraged. You can do this.

Chapter 11

How to Open Escrow

Once the offer is accepted and signed by all parties, you need to open escrow right away. It can be done by you or the buyer.

To open escrow, take the contract and the earnest money deposit check to the escrow / title company you or the buyer chose.

Connect with the escrow officer and she / he will open escrow and give you an escrow number.

The buyer can open escrow too, just make sure everyone has the escrow number from the escrow agent.

The escrow agent will order a title search to make sure your title is free and clear. Sometimes it is not.

The escrow agent will advise you what needs to be done if the title is not clear.

Know that the escrow agent is not a real estate agent and will be 100% impartial. The escrow agent's duty is to read the contract and perform according to what the contract dictates. If you missed anything, the escrow agent will ask you, but you can't say, "I don't know, what do you think?"

An escrow agent is prohibited from giving you advice. It is highly advisable to not discuss the transaction with others during the escrow.

You might receive another offer. If so, just accept pending the sale you have going. You can say to a second offer, "The transaction is supposed to close on this date. If something goes wrong and it won't close, your offer will be next in line." Don't discuss the terms of the offer you already have. Just look at the offer and do the math. Write a counteroffer if you don't like what you have received. Don't rush, but don't procrastinate either. Always sleep on it, always. Instant acceptance or denial never works well.

Be sure that you have a prequalification letter from the second buyer, too. Inform the buyer that you are in escrow with ASAP that you have a backup offer. Explain that if the escrow doesn't close by the agreed upon time, the contract will be null and void and the new offer will take precedent. Inform the escrow officer, too, and be sure to tell the loan officer. Loan officers might need an extension. Be careful with this. Only agree to any extension with sufficient proof that the loan can be finalized. You don't want to lose the next buyer.

You could receive multiple offers in the same day. That is a situation most people say, "is a wish come true!". It's not. Be very careful with this one. You should immediately tell all buyers that you received multiple offers and give them 24 hours to submit their highest and best offer, no other details like " I need an offer above this price", or "I need a full price offer. Just say "Property is subject to multiple offers. All buyers to submit their highest and best offer by this particular date".

At the end of 24 hours, put all offers on your table and calculate each one. Also look at how it will be paid.

If a cash offer is on the table, it needs to be looked at first because it will close faster. However, it might be a lot lower than the other offers. You need to calculate all closing costs and inspection fees. Calculate, review and sleep on it, then decide and sign. Sign the offer you accept and the one(s) you reject. Sign the rejected offers and write rejected. I would also select two options, your first and second. Ask the second offer if they would agree with a second position. If yes, proceed with giving the first position buyer a 30 or 45 day close of escrow and tell them you have a second position.

Chapter 12

INSPECTIONS AND APPRAISAL

Once escrow is open, time is of the essence. You only have the timeframes everyone agreed to in the contract. Any timeframe missed can cause the contract to void. Contract terms need to be followed by both parties, buyer(s) and seller(s).

Inspections need to be ordered and are best if ordered by the buyer. I'm not saying paid for by the buyer but ordered by buyer - no matter who will pay. Doing so releases the seller from potential liability, meaning the buyer can't say the seller has a friendship with the inspector and so on. The buyer can be there when the inspector is there, but it is best if the seller is not there.

If you are there, do NOT say a word. Find something to do outside. Let the inspector inspect. If you start "bugging" into the inspector's business, you completely release the inspector from liability. Inspectors write down everything that gets said during inspections, and if complaints happen, the inspector will say, "seller (or buyer) was present and raised himself/

herself as a pro, telling me how to do my job." Best to not have any comments or suggestions. This is very important!

The inspector will distribute the report to the buyer, and the buyer can send it to the seller. If the buyer requests repairs, I suggest you ask them to give you the inspection report.

You can negotiate the repairs if the buyer asks you to repair something you don't want to. You can ask the buyer how much they will want in exchange for the repairs and write an addendum to the contract. Say, "In lieu of repairs (itemize each one), seller agrees to credit buyer at close of escrow this (specific) dollar amount." Or you can repair it yourself or have a contractor come and repair it. You have to ask the buyer if they are OK with you doing repairs yourself. If you hire a licensed professional, you might or might not have to pay the repair costs at the time of service. Some contractors will bill escrow. In that case, you will give out the escrow number and escrow officer's name.

Once the inspections are done, send the inspection report to escrow, too. If you have a house with well and septic, you might be required to have them inspected. They might also ask you for a survey. Follow the same rules as above, meaning have the buyer order inspections and stay out of the way. You can find more details at the end of the book in the inspection forms.

Chapter 13

CONTINGENCIES AND REMOVAL

All inspections are done, repairs are done, and buyers are happy and accept everything. Now you need to have the buyer sign a contingency removal form. All parties sign and date the form, then send it to escrow.

Capture the specific contingencies, the deadlines they are to be removed, and any reminders or notes you want to keep in the space below.

Contingency	Deadline for removal	Notes

Chapter 14

CLOSING ESCROW

The loan officer is almost done with the loan. It is imperative to keep attention on the loan during the whole process. Ask for weekly updates. Note: You didn't sell your house until the escrow officer calls you and tells you, "Congratulations! We closed."

Once all inspections are done, all contingencies removed, and the loan is approved, the escrow will start with the closing process. You will be asked to sign and so will the buyer. Once the loan is approved it will fund and close, usually within 48 business hours. The exact time will be provided to you by the escrow officer.

It is not advised to move out until the loan is fully approved. There are too many issues that can happen with a loan, and at the very last minute you can hear, "Sorry, the loan is not going through." If you have a place to move to before you sell the house, do so, but don't move out everything. Leave some furniture for the last minute, just in case it doesn't close, and you have to start from scratch. You want to avoid having a vacant home.

Remember, a sale gone sideways can happen with or without a real estate agent involved. The good part in a sale gone sideways is that you already have all inspections done and know exactly how to perform next time. It is very annoying, but it happens more than we want it to. That's why you have to get updates from the loan officer. Usually the earnest money deposit will cover the inspections, unless all were paid at the time of closing. If that's the case, the escrow officer will pay inspections and cancel escrow.

Note: When you get the message that the loan is approved and all documents are signed, many buyer(s) want to start moving things in.

Do NOT accept this!

The reason I'm saying this is because your home insurance might not cover them as future buyers, and if something happens, bad stuff can come out of it. Just let them wait until they get the key from you.

They can receive the key from you right after the closing.

Chapter 15

MOVING OUT

Two days before escrow closes, you need to have the walkthrough. That's when the buyers come and check to see if everything is still there and in working condition. They might also take some time to measure rooms and walls. Have them sign and date the walkthrough form.

When your escrow agent tells you that the loan is ap- proved and funded, that's when you can move out.

You have to be ready and have the movers planned. Have a cleaning crew planned.

Leave the property clean, and make sure all trash is gone.

Don't forget to leave garage door openers, appliance paperwork, phone numbers on utilities, or any other services for the property.

If the new buyer is not local, this is a big service and not a big deal for a seller. Leave any information you think they might need.

Give them a thank you card, even if they don't deserve it. It is good for you to leave in harmony.

After the closing day (not earlier), cancel all utilities you have in your name, and if possible, transfer to seller. Usually just telling the companies the new owner's name will do it. That way the new owner won't be burdened with shut offs.

Cancel all services you had on the property, like lawncare, pool care, and so on. Change the address with these services to your new one.

Use the space below to capture your personal list of moving out chores and notes.

_____

_____

_____

_____

_____

_____

_____

_____

_____

Congratulations!

YOU SOLD YOUR HOUSE!

Moving checklist

Remember to pack a bag with necessary items for the moving time!

Change of address:

- Post office
- Credit cards and other accounts
- Subscriptions
- Family and Friends

Bank accounts:

- Cancel auto payments
- Arrange banking in your new location
- Check your safety deposit box

Insurance:

- Notify all insurance companies of your new location

Set up new utilities:

- Gas Electric Water Phone
- Fuel/propane Garbage Cable

Pets:

- Ask vet for records, vaccinations, tags

Children:

- Register for new school Transfer school records Arrange for day care Doctors/dentists
- Transfer current prescriptions
- Obtain records (birth, medical, x-rays)

New address:

- Set up utilities before your first night
- Check on pilot lights
- Change your driver's license
- Register your car
- Register to vote

Meet with potential new doctors

Chapter 16

OWNER CARRY TERMS

If you own your home free and clear, meaning you don't have a loan against it, you can sell with owner carry terms. That means you can have a contract similar to what a bank does and receive payments. This option should be taken with a lot of caution.

Here are a few things to know:

Buyer's credit report: You need to ask the buyer to supply you with a current credit report. Everybody can get their own report online. You need to read it and find out if there are any delinquencies or charge offs. This is important because if the credit suggests such things, the borrower could do them to you, too.

Down payment: You need to receive at least a 20% down payment. Otherwise there is "no skin in the game." You also need to ask where the money comes from. If they get the money from someone else and will have to pay it back, that might make the payment to you less affordable.

Interest rate: You need to ask for an interest rate comparable to current interest rates in order to not violate lending laws.

You need to think about how many years you'd like to have the money locked up. Do you want to receive payments for 30 years? If not, you can suggest you carry for 5 or 7 or 10 years, amortized for 30 years and payable in full without prepayment penalty. Don't get greedy and ask for a prepayment penalty. Prepayment penalty means that if the borrower pays the loan off early it will cost them a penalty. Most banks no longer do that.

You need to think about what you are going to do when they become delinquent. Many people say, "I'll just take the house back." That's true but also very time consuming and expensive. You need to know the foreclosure laws in your state and follow them to the letter, including proper notifications when delinquency starts and many other details. This is very important! People get behind all the time, and, many people know how to use the foreclosure law system.

If you decide to go the owner carry route, follow the contract terms as we discussed and write "owner carry" in the loan section. You need to specify where the payments will go and the terms. You should include how many days they can be late and what will happen when they're late. I would suggest a note servicing company, and the buyer should pay the fees. I have worked with Evergreen Note Servicing. They set up an account and the payments go to them. They send you the money when it arrives and keep flawless records. They DO NOT send out late payment notices. You have to do that. There are other loan servicing companies, just ask the escrow officer for recommendation.

Here is the Dodd Frank act that applies to owner financing:

https://barneswalker.com/seller-financing-restrictions-under-the-dodd-frank-act/

Chapter 17

Reverse Mortgages

A reverse mortgage was implemented for people who don't want to move but need money to live on. It is what the title implies – a loan – but you don't have to pay it back until later, or after death, depending on which option you choose.

You have to be 62 or older, meaning everyone who is on the title of the house needs to be that age.

You have to have a good amount of equity in your home or have it paid off.

You don't have to have an income to qualify. There are several options, and none are cheap.

You have to go to a HUD approved reverse mortgage counselor, also called HECM counselor, before you decide. This is now required.

You should truly understand what you're getting into!

Have the counselor write down details for you. It is best if you discuss your decision with someone else, too, a family member or friend.

Here are a few web sites with more information.

https://reverse.org/

https://www.aarp.org/money/credit-loans-debt/info-2019/reverse-mortgage-loan-advice.html

Chapter 18

SELLING YOUR HOME WITH A REALTOR

So, you've read this book and decided, nah, you would much rather hire someone to help. That's okay. Here is what you need to do.

The first and most important step is to make sure you and everyone living with you truly want to sell the house. This is not a joke: if anyone who owns the

property holds on to it in his/her heart, the house will not sell. So, take this seriously and make sure everyone is on the same page, meaning everyone has come to an agreement to sell and move on to a new venture. Clean and declutter the house and property. This is more important than having the home updated.

Choosing an agent to represent you:

Check around your neighborhood for homes that are listed for sale. Note the agent whose name shows up on the most properties. They will be your first option because that is most likely the agent that knows the area and how to sell your home. If you don't like that agent for whatever reason, look up the most active agency in your immediate area.

Make a call and ask to interview agents to list your home. You can also call the local Real Estate Association and ask for a Realtor who is active in the area.

You will get a lot of responses. Schedule appointments and interview them. Ask them specifically what they will do to advertise and sell your property. Ask how much experience they have in selling a home like yours and how many years they've been in business. Ask if they are an agent or a Realtor. A Realtor is an agent who is a member of the National Association of Realtors and adheres to duties created to serve you in the most honest way. An agent who is not a Realtor is not a member and cannot advertise your property on Realtor.com. I don't suggest hiring an agent who is not a Realtor.

Ask a lot of questions until you feel comfortable with someone. Many people shy away from new Realtors. Truth is, a new Realtor will go above and beyond to sell your home and will have more help from a broker. The truth is also that they don't have the experience to negotiate. You can ask to lower the commission because they're new.

Go with whom you feel you can trust, but make sure you tell them you will fire them if they don't do what is promised. Don't lock yourself into a long-term contract. List for a few months and tell them you will extend if needed. Don't go by who tells you they can sell at a high price. If the price is not realistic, the property will not sell.

If you have a home with acreage, a ranch, or a high-end home, you really need to **not** rush into choosing a Realtor.

A home with septic and well needs an agent that has a lot of prior experience with such properties in that area. That's a must. No exceptions.

Same with a high-end home. Find an agent who either lives or has a lot of prior experience in that area. Interview and interview more until you feel confident about who you would like to work with.

In either case, do not agree with buyer and seller representation. You are the one who should be represented by your agent, not both.

Dual representation is still legal in many states, but it is highly discouraged by most brokers.

Chapter 19

VITAL INFORMATION FOR THE PROCESS

The following pages contain vital information you need to successfully sell your home.

- Helpful and Important Links
- How to Write a Contract (with examples)
- List of Inspections
- Title and Closing Costs
- Seller Real Property Disclosure
- Fair Housing

HELPFUL AND IMPORTANT LINKS

Print a contract for your state. This resource is free for one week:

https://www.lawdepot.com/contracts/real-estate-purchase-agreement

Fair Housing Act:

https://www.hud.gov/program_offices/fair_housing_equal_opp/fair_housing_act_overview

Flood insurance:

https://www.fema.gov/national-flood-insurance-program

HOW TO WRITE A CONTRACT

(examples)

Residential offer and acceptance agreement

Received from (buyers name) ....

Price of $ US Dollars .... type numbers and spell the amount

For the property located at .... address, city, county

APN ....

Earnest money deposit......$ 1000.00 evidenced by check to be made out to escrow. Company name .... write company name here.................

Escrow officer name .... write officer name here .... to be deposited within 24 hours of acceptance.

Balance of cash down payment, not including closing costs .... write the amount here ....
(This number is to be taken from buyer's loan officer.)

Source of down payment .... (This is important because if you hear "my friend," or "my mom will
give me the money," it is a red flag. They might not get
a loan.)

Cash purchase .... (If you have a cash
buyer, here is where you need to say so.) ....
Buyers to provide evidence of sufficient cash available
to complete this purchase within 5 business days of
acceptance. The evidence can be a signed letter from
the bank where they have the funds.

A print-out from the internet or a statement is not
enough; it can be fake. If you have this scenario and
you don't receive proof of funds, the contract is null
and void.

Don't start with any inspections before the 5 days. You
DO have to open escrow within 1 business day.

Loan proceeds .... write here the total loan
amount .... (This is if the buyer needs to take
out a loan or two.)

What kind of loan are they taking out? Call and ask
their loan officer, but it should be listed on the preapproval letter.

This is important because if the loan officer changes
the loan from conventional to FHA or VA, you will
have extra charges. If the loan terms are in this contract

and everyone signed and dated it, in case of change of terms, you can void the contract. If they intend to take out two loans, that needs to be specified as well.

Write exactly what the preapproval letter states.

If you have a buyer who wants to take out FHA or VA loans, stop here and ask the loan officer what concessions they expect from you. You need to know that and calculate it in your bottom line.

Sale of other property .... this is in case you receive an offer contingent on the buyer selling their home. If that's the case, include: This agreement is contingent upon conveyance of buyer's property described as .... write address here, due to close by .... write the date the buyer gives you.

If the buyer says, "I don't know," that's not OK. You have to come up with a date or you will have an open contract, which is not a strong contract.

If you are in this scenario, write here; If the escrow on the contingent property doesn't close by (date) this agreement will terminate unless buyer and seller agree in writing to extend.

This is a hard to work with scenario, but unfortunately, it happens a lot. If the buyer's house is already in escrow and due to close soon, that's okay and is easier to deal with. If it is not in escrow or even on the market, I would suggest you don't accept. You can tell them to come back when they're in escrow.

Closing: close of escrow to be ………….. write the date here ……………

Appraisal: buyer to pay for appraisal ……………… (Seldom will a seller pay for an appraisal, but if you agree to pay for it, write it here.)

Inspections to be completed within …………………. usually 15 days of acceptance but can be longer.

Inspections to be ordered by …………… specify if buyer or seller, meaning this is the party who will choose and make appointments with inspectors. If the buyer wants to do that, they need to agree to coordinate with seller.

LIST OF INSPECTIONS

Here is a list of inspections you might have to deal with: Choose what you have and decide who pays for what. Be specific and have the buyer initial each one.

- Pest inspection
- Home inspection
- Heating system inspection
- Cooling system inspection
- Survey
- Well quality
- Well quantity
- Septic pumping
- Septic inspection
- Septic lid location and exposure
- Fireplace inspection
- Woodburning stove
- Oil tank test

Other inspections .... List any additional inspections here.

_____

_____

_____

_____

_____

Here is a list of other items you might have to deal with: Again, decide who pays for what. Be specific and have the buyer initial each one.

Reinspection .... this is in case the inspector needs to come back and reinspect what was repaired. Decide who will pay for that and specify here. The fee is usually a bit less than the original inspection.

Repairs: You need to put a cap on the amount of money you want to spend on repairs. I can't give you a number suggestion because it depends on what needs to be done. Putting a cap is necessary for your own best interest. It will make the buyer set priorities for what they truly want to have repaired and not go crazy with every little thing. Write: seller will pay up to .... towards repairs.

Association fees and transfer fees.........write here if you have an association and who pays.

Bonds and assessments: If there are any other bonds or assessments, specify who pays.

Extras :

If you have solar energy or any other alternative that needs to be paid for or that is already paid for, specify.

If you have personal property that you would like to leave, specify (like a hot tub or above the ground pool).

If you have any proposed installations that you know of, like a water meter, that the well might be subject to be connected to a public water system, you're aware that a new development is proposed near the property, or anything else that the buyer needs to know, address that.

TITLE AND CLOSING COSTS

Seller will pay for standard owner's policy of title insurance. This is common.

Buyer to pay for lender's policy. This is common.

Escrow fee ....…...... this can be split equally or paid by one or the other. Specify.

Transfer tax ....…..... this can also be either split or paid by one party. Specify.

Home warranty. If the buyer wants a home warranty, let them buy it. Don't choose a home warranty for them, even if you decide to pay. There are various packages, and they all have strings attached. Let the buyer deal with that.

Final walkthrough: Give the buyer the right to see the property prior to close of escrow. Agree on a date here, usually a few days before closing date.

SELLER REAL PROPERTY DISCLOSURE

Here is a list of things you should address. Check if you have done so and check if there are issues with any of them. Address each one and disclose any trouble you have or have had in the past.

- Plumbing Electrical system Sewer lines
- Sewer system Septic tank Leach field
- Well
- Well pump Sprinkler system Fountain
- Heating system
- Solar system
- Cooling system
- Fireplace and chimney
- Wood burning stove
- Water treatment system
- Water heater
- Toilets
- Bathtubs

- Sinks
- Showers
- Sauna
- Hot tub
- Built-in microwave (If it is built-in you need to leave it; if it is stand alone, you can negotiate.)
- Range oven
- Hood fan
- Dishwasher
- Garbage disposal
- Trash compactor
- Central vacuum
- Alarm system (Is it owned or leased?)
- Smoke detectors (You need to have them.)
- Intercom
- Data communication lines
- Satellite equipment
- Other ....

You need to address any issues you have or had in the past, whether they were repaired or not.

- Any water damages
- Any structural issues

- Any modifications, alterations or repairs, especially if made without a permit.

- Any construction defects

- Any foundation settlement

- Any trouble with the soil or drainage Any encroachments or easements Any problems with the roof

- Any mold problems

- Any termites, carpenter ants or other infestations

- Any environmental hazard such as but not limited to asbestos, radon gas, urea formaldehyde, fuel or chemical storage tanks

- Any Methamphetamine manufactured on the property

- Any shared use of the property like fences, walls, or driveways

- Any lead-based paint

Any other items................

Add anything else that might need to be known to a buyer. Both parties, buyers and sellers, need to sign and date.

Everyone has to sign and date every page. If you forget this step, you don't have a contract!

FAIR HOUSING

The Fair Housing Act was created and made into law to prevent discrimination. The Civil Act of 1968 contained the Fair Housing Act legislation, which was later modified by the Fair Housing Amendments Act of 1988. There are seven classes protected by the Federal Fair Housing Act. They are:

- Race
- Color
- Religion
- National Origin
- Sex
- Handicap
- Familial Status

Many states have passed their own laws regarding discrimination. The state of California, for example, expanded the protected classes in its own Fair Housing legislation. The protected classes under the California Fair Employment and Housing Act stem from the

Unruh Civil Rights Act of 1959 and prohibit discrimination based on:

- Age
- Ancestry
- Arbitrary discrimination
- Gender expression or Gender identity
- Genetic Information
- Marital Status
- Medical Condition
- Sexual Orientation
- Source of Income

Do NOT use these words:

- Sports-minded
- Bachelor Apartment
- Professional
- Mother-in-Law Quarters
- Couples
- Singles Only
- Mature
- Married
- Seniors

- Gentleman's Farm
- Golden Agers
- Section 8
- Integrated
- Handicapped
- Children Welcome

Safe Neighborhood – Don't discuss neighborhood crime. If asked, tell potential buyers to check the crime watch website for the area.

GLOSSARY OF TERMS

Acre- a measurement of land equal to 43,560 square feet.

Adjusted cost basis- the cost of improvements the seller makes to the property. Deducting the cost from the original sales price provides the profit or loss of a home when it is sold.

Appraisal value- an opinion of a property's fair market value, based on appraiser's knowledge, experience, analysis of the property, and comparable sales.

Assessed value- a valuation placed on property by a public tax assessor for purpose of taxation.

Assessment- the placing of a value on property for the purpose of taxation.

Assignment- when ownership of your mortgage is transferred to another.

Assumable mortgage- a mortgage that can be assumed by the buyer when a home is sold. Usually, the borrower must qualify in order to assume the loan. This is an option that has almost disappeared and is no longer offered.

Chain of title- an analysis of the transfers of title to a piece of property over the years.

Clear title- a title that is free of liens or legal questions as to ownership of the property.

Closing- this has different meanings in different states. In some states a real estate transaction is not closed until the documents are recorded at the local recorder's office. In others, the "closing" is a meeting where

all of the documents are signed and money changes hands.

Closing costs- closing costs are separated into what

are called "non-recurring closing costs" and "pre-paid items."

Non-recurring closing costs are items which are paid once.

Pre-paids are items which recur over time, such as property taxes and homeowner's insurance.

A lender makes an attempt to estimate the amount of non-recurring closing costs and prepaid items on the Good Faith Estimate, which they must issue to the borrower within three days of receiving a home loan application.

Cloud on title- any conditions revealed by a title search that adversely affect the title to a real estate. Usually clouds cannot be removed except by deed, release, or court action.

Co-borrower- an additional individual who is both obligated on the loan and is on the title to the property.

Collection- when a borrower falls behind, the lender contacts them in an effort to bring the loan current. The loan goes to collection. As part of the collection effort, the lender must mail and record certain documents in case they are eventually required to foreclose.

Common Area Assessments or Homeowners Association fees- charges paid to the homeowner's associations by the owners of the individual units in a planned unit development (PUD) and which are generally used to maintain some parts of the property and common areas.

Comparable sales- recent sales of similar properties in nearby areas, often used to determine the market value of a property. Also referred to as "comps."

Contingency- a condition that must be met before a contract is legally binding. For example, home buyers often include a contingency that specifies that the contract is not binding until the seller provides a home inspection report from a qualified inspector.

Deed-in-lieu- short for deed-in-lieu of foreclosure. This conveys title to the lender when the borrower is in default and wants to avoid foreclosure. The lender may or may not cease foreclosure activities if a borrower asks to provide a deed-in-lieu. Regardless of whether the lender accepts the deed-in-lieu, the avoidance and non-repayment of debt will most likely show on a credit history. What a deed-in-lieu might prevent is having the documents preparatory to a foreclosure being recorded and becoming a matter of public record.

Deed of trust- some states don't record mortgages.

Instead, they record a deed of trust, which is essentially the same thing.

Earnest money deposit- a deposit made by the potential buyer to show they are serious about buying the property.

Easement- a right of way giving persons other than the owner access to or over a property.

Eminent domain- the right of a government to take private property for public use upon payment of its fair market value. Eminent domain is the basis for condemnation proceedings.

Encroachment- an improvement that intrudes illegally on another's property.

Encumbrance- anything that affects or limits the fee simple title to a property, such as mortgages, easements, or restrictions.

Equal Credit Opportunity Act (ECOA)- a federal law that requires lenders and other creditors to make credit equally available without discrimination based on race, color, religion, national origin, age, sex, marital status, or receipt of income from public programs.

Equity- a homeowner's financial interest in a property. Equity is the difference between the fair market value of the property owned and the amount still owed on its mortgage and other liens.

Escrow- an item of value, money, or documents deposited with a third party to be delivered upon the fulfillment of a condition.

Fixture- personal property that becomes real property when attached in a permanent manner to a real estate.

Home warranty- a type of insurance that covers repairs to certain parts of a house and some fixtures.

Lead- a metallic chemical element present in older dwellings, primarily in the form of lead-based paint and lead plumbing. Exposure to lead has been found to be a health risk.

Transfer tax- an assessment by state or local authorities at the time a property changes hands.

R-Value- a construction term that refers to the resistance of heat loss. The higher the R Value, the slower the rate of heat loss.

Radon- a ground generated radioactive gas that seeps into some homes through sump pumps, cracks in the foundation and other inlets. A leading cause of lung cancer.

Tap fee- most companies charge a tap fee for hooking up utilities.

Congratulations!

You just learned the process of selling your home!

ABOUT THE AUTHOR

With nearly 20 years' experience as a professional Realtor, Jeni has helped hundreds of people buy homes, land, farms, ranches and investment properties until she retired from real estate sales in 2019. She served at not only the local and state levels on various real estate committees, but at the national and global level.

Born in Romania and spending 10 years of her life in Germany, Jeni arrived in the USA in 1988 and purchased her first home in 1989, birthing her education in real estate investing. She has purchased and sold 21 homes and 11 parcels of land for her own family and for investment purposes, making a profit on each and every one.

Jeni's bigger vision for northern Nevada was put into motion with her leadership in working with REALTORS® to understand cultural differences in buying and selling real estate locally and internationally. She was involved with the Governors' Office on Economic Development and the Northern Nevada Developmental Authority and served as the chair of the Reno/Sparks Association of REALTORS® Global Business Committee. As a Global Presidential Liaison and a Real estate teacher to REALTORS® worldwide, Jeni brought global real estate investment education to Northern Nevada and received the prestigious Abraham Curry Award in 2015.

She served for five years as the National Association of REALTORS® Presidential Liaison to Romania. With her help, Romania is one of the first Eastern European countries to adopt the principles of organized real estate including the REALTOR® Code of Ethics and a Multiple Listing Service.

Jeni studied various schools of feng shui and chose western feng shui for real estate, which she actively used in each and every real estate transaction, both for herself and for her clients. Feng Shui is the language of harmony. Once you understand it, harmony will always be with you. You don't need to believe in it to experience the benefits.

Have you ever noticed how most prices end with the number "99"? Some examples are $8.99 and 99.99. This is because 9 is the best and luckiest number of all numbers and pricing this way helps make items sell. Numbers, energy and personal directions are all huge influences in our lives and can help us succeed (or create messes with our health, money and happiness).

When you buy a house that is out of harmony with your own energy, you can lose money, get sick, or have something else that is troubling happen. We can make a conscious effort to live in harmony with our environment and eliminate bad energy by balancing our environment with simple Feng Shui remedies. It actually **is** simple, once we know what to look for.

During the economic downturn in 2008, she became a Hud approved housing counselor and opened a counseling office in Reno. Securing this license required extensive HUD approved education in finances, foreclosure and default counseling, first time home buyer education, renters' laws, credit counseling and reverse mortgage.

Jeni earned many certifications as a leader in real estate, including:

- Real Estate Broker Licensed in Nevada
- Certified International Property Specialist
- Commercial Real Estate
- Business Broker
- Certified Eco Broker (Association of Energy and Environmental Real Estate)
- NeighborWorks Certified Housing Counselor
- HECM- Reverse Mortgage counselor
- Foreclosure Intervention and Default Counselor

- REO certified (real estate owned)
- Bridges Out of Poverty Trainer

She also holds certifications as a Life Coach, Health Coach, and Financial Coach. She has served clients in her capacities as a Foreclosure Intervention and Default Counselor, Certified Loss Mitigation Advisor, Credit Counselor, and Financial Social Worker.

Jeni leads a very busy life but is never too busy to help someone achieve their own success.

She offers the following services:

Credit repair class delivered via phone or internet

You've likely heard of companies that promise to erase the bad credit items from your report to improve your score. They charge several hundred and there is **never** a guarantee (if you read the fine print). You will learn step by step how they do that and receive all the forms to do it yourself.

Contact Jeni at coach@RMoneyClub.com for details.

Feng Shui/Numerology personal analysis

Receive your very own analysis to use forever in everything you do. This includes

- Your personal numbers to use in real estate or anything you do

- Luckiest colors to wear
- Instructions for your home and remedies for successful living
- Your personal sitting and sleeping directions for success
- How to live with your partner or other people living in the same house
- Plus answers to your personal questions

If you'd like your life to go your way, you need to go Feng Shui! Contact Jeni at coach@RMoneyClub.com for details.

Real Estate investing coaching

Every successful person (or most of them) made significant profits in real estate investing. I did too! I can help you be a successful real estate investor even if you don't have a huge amount of money to start with.

Coaching is delivered in a small group webinar or one on one. Reading both books I authored is a prerequisite (this book and *"How to Buy a Home That Makes You Happy"*).

You can learn more at https://www.RMoneyClub.com/ or email me at Coach@RMoneyClub.com.

A Special Bonus from Jeni

Now that you've read *For Sale By Owner*, you are on your way to understanding exactly how you can sell your home for the most money you can get at the time you want to sell it, with or without a Realtor. You can now forget the fear of selling your home and put the profit in your own pocket!

You'll also receive the special bonus I created to add to your toolkit ... The *FSBO Toolkit*, which includes:

- List of key resources links you will need for success in selling your home (with links for direct access)
- Seller Real Property Disclosure form
- Special pricing on classes and offerings. See below for details.

This *FSBO Toolkit* is offered as a special bonus to this book's readers, and you can claim it for free here:

https://www.rmoneyclub.com/toolkit

Did you know you can begin real estate investing, even if you don't have a lot of money? No get rich fast scheme...just sound, professional coaching to help you achieve your financial independence. Email me at Coach@RMoneyClub.com for your special pricing.

Did you know that interest rates on any loan is directly tied to your credit report? Optimize your credit with a credit repair class. Email me at Coach@RMoneyClub.com for your special pricing.

Did you know Feng Shui in your home is an invisible influence on your health, wealth, and overall happiness? Order a personalize Feng Shui analysis with special pricing. Just go to https://www.rmoneyclub.com/.

I'm in your corner. Let me know if I can help further.

Here's to the successful sale of your home!

Best,
Jeni